Tom Woo

Getting Started on the Trumpet

beginning and intermediate studies

first edition

Center Stage Publishing

Printed in the United States of America

ISBN 978-1-7360876-0-2

First Printing, 2017

Center Stage Publishing
P.O. Box 622
Mountain View, CA 94042

www.takecenterstage.today

Contents

Who Should Use This Book

This book is best for musicians at the beginner levels that are learning with a teacher. If you are returning to trumpet after a long time off or are more advanced, you could also use it as a way to review what you know and and to get back in shape. For more advanced players, there is *Progressive Scale and Arpeggio Studies and* other standard method books.

How To Use This Book

Having started as a way to have some scales, arpeggios, and musical examples in every key all in one place, this book is meant to be a tool to go with any typical way of learning trumpet. It can be a way to ease into other standard method books that may seem more advanced.

The book is not meant to be read from cover to cover like a novel. Each "part" has material that you can progress through, gradually getting used to playing various patterns and sequences in all key signatures. Many of the examples from classical music are in their original key, even if it might be a "hard" or "bad" key for trumpet, so that you can hear how it might sound in concert and in case you'd like to play along with a recording of the piece.

Why Scales, Arpeggios, and Basic Melodies?

One way to really enjoy trumpet playing is by reaching a point where you can play the music you enjoy without being hindered by and preoccupied with mechanics. To get there, it helps to gain the "muscle memory" of many musical patterns, so that you really do not have to think about them. A great way to do this is to practice scales, arpeggios, and basic melodies in all key signatures.

Here are a few suggestions:

- For each study, start with a tempo that lets you to play with accurate pitches and rhythms while keeping the tempo steady. Then, gradually increase the tempo from there.
- Play the scales and arpeggios in various styles and volumes and with various articulations, including completely slurred.
- As you improve, play the exercises in octaves other than the ones written.
- Don't avoid the exercises written in (seemingly) "difficult" keys. They won't seem that difficult after you spend some time with them, and the long-term payoff is significant.

As you progress, you might find the tips and suggestions marked with this icon to be useful.

The music in this book is an early step in a trumpet player's journey. I hope that it gives you some part of a solid foundation that enables you to approach all the great musical opportunities in the world with confidence.

Have fun!

First Notes

Study 1.1

If you are new to the trumpet, you can use these simple scales to get started on making a good sound and coordinating the valves.

C · D · E · F · G

0 ← fingerings → 1/3 · 1/2 · 1 · 0

time signature
(See Appendix for more information.)

Study 1.2

A · B · C · D · E

1/2 · 2 · 0 · 1/3 · 1/2

Study 1.3

key signature
(See Appendix for more information.)

Study 1.4

Study 1.5

Here you can get used to changing between notes that are farther apart.

Study 1.6

Basic Scales

Study 2.1A
major

C# Major

D♭ Major

A♭ Major

E♭ Major

B♭ Major

F Major

C Major

More About Fingerings for Low D and Low C#/D♭

D

extend the 3rd valve slide a bit

C#   D♭

extend the 3rd valve slide a lot

At first, just get used to using the 3rd valve slide while pressing the valves. Then, work with an experienced trumpeter and maybe a tuner to find out the best slide positions for your trumpet to be in tune on these pitches.

Study 2.1B
natural minor

A Minor

E Minor

B Minor

F# Minor

C# Minor

G# Minor

Ab Minor

D# Minor

Eb Minor

A# Minor

B♭ Minor

F Minor

C Minor

G Minor

D Minor

A Minor

Basic Scales

Study 2.2A
major

C Major

G Major

D Major

A Major

E Major

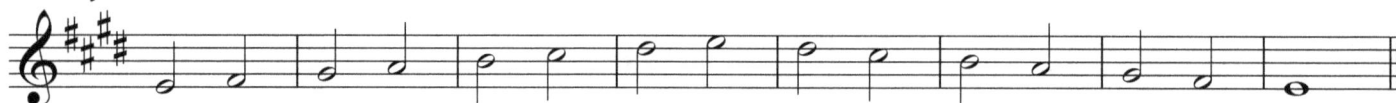

B Major

C♭ Major

F♯ Major

G♭ Major

C♯ Major

D♭ Major

A♭ Major

E♭ Major

B♭ Major

F Major

C Major

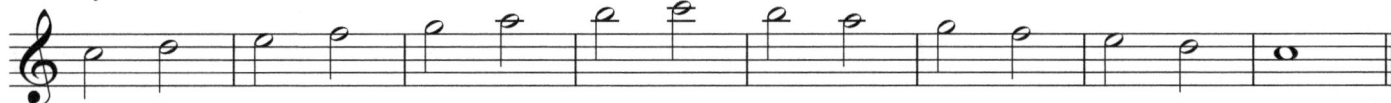

Start with octaves that are comfortable, but work toward playing each scale in multiple octaves.

Study 2.2B
natural minor

A Minor

E Minor

B Minor

F# Minor

C# Minor

G# Minor

Ab Minor

D# Minor

Eb Minor

A♯ Minor

B♭ Minor

F Minor

C Minor

G Minor

D Minor

A Minor

Basic Scales

Study 2.3A
major

This scale rhythm is good to know for school and honor band auditions.

C Major

G Major

D Major

A Major

E Major

B Major

Cb Major

F# Major

Gb Major

C# Major

Db Major

Ab Major

Eb Major

Bb Major

F Major

C Major

Variation

Articulation Suggestions

Study 2.3B
melodic minor

A Minor

raised 6th and 7th

It is common for music in minor keys to have the 6th and 7th scale degrees
raised a half-step in certain situations. (See Appendix for more information.)

E Minor

B Minor

F♯ Minor

C♯ Minor

Double-sharps raise a pitch by a whole-step.
double-sharp (See Appendix for more information on **whole-steps**.)

G♯ Minor

A♭ Minor

D♯ Minor

E♭ Minor

A# Minor

Bb Minor

F Minor

C Minor

G Minor

D Minor

A Minor

Variation

Articulation Suggestions

Study 2.4A
major

This is another scale rhythm that is good to know for school and honor band auditions.

C Major

9th scale degree
(See Appendix for more information on *scale degrees*.)

G Major

D Major

A Major

E Major

B Major

C♭ Major

F♯ Major

G♭ Major

C# Major

D♭ Major

A♭ Major

E♭ Major

B♭ Major

F Major

C Major

Variation

Articulation Suggestions

Basic Scales

Study 2.4B
melodic minor

A Minor

E Minor

B Minor

F# Minor

C# Minor

G# Minor

Ab Minor

D# Minor

Eb Minor

A# Minor

B♭ Minor

F Minor

C Minor

G Minor

D Minor

A Minor

Variation

Articulation Suggestions

Basic Arpeggios

Study 3.1A
major

C Major

G Major

D Major

A Major

E Major

B Major

C♭ Major

F♯ Major

G♭ Major

C# Major

Db Major

Ab Major

Eb Major

Bb Major

F Major

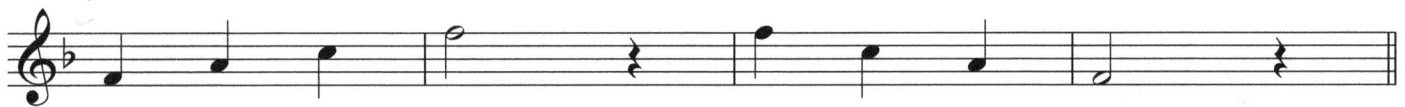

C Major

Be careful not to tighten your lips too much on the way up or loosen them too much on the way down. Aim for the best sound on each note.

Basic Arpeggios

Study 3.1B
minor

A Minor

E Minor

B Minor

F# Minor

C# Minor

G# Minor

Ab Minor

D# Minor

Eb Minor

A# Minor

B♭ Minor

F Minor

C Minor

G Minor

D Minor

A Minor

Study 3.2A
major

C Major

G Major

D Major

A Major

E Major

B Major

C♭ Major

F♯ Major

G♭ Major

C# Major

Db Major

Ab Major

Eb Major

Bb Major

F Major

C Major

Basic Arpeggios

Study 3.2B
minor

A Minor

E Minor

B Minor

F# Minor

C# Minor

G# Minor

Ab Minor

D# Minor

Eb Minor

A♯ Minor

B♭ Minor

F Minor

C Minor

G Minor

D Minor

A Minor

Beginning Melodies

Getting Started

Moving Along

Jumping Around

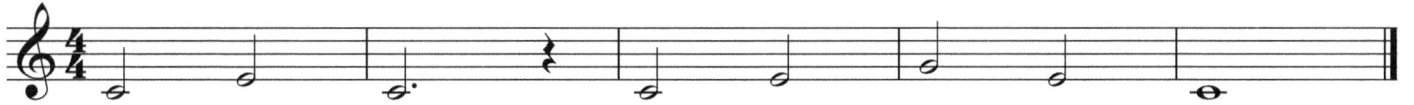

"Hot Crossed Buns"

Traditional

Traditional

"Go Tell Aunt Rhody"

Beginning Melodies

"Mary Had a Little Lamb"

♩ = 96 - 120

Traditional

"Twinkle Twinkle Little Star"

♩ = 96 - 120

Traditional

"Frère Jacques"

♩ = 96 - 120

Traditional

Time to Rest

♩ = 96 - 120

"Old MacDonald"

♩ = 108 - 132

"This Old Man"

♩ = 108 - 132

Variations on "Twinkle Twinkle Little Star"

♩ = 96 - 120

Dotted Quarter Chant

Dotted Quarter Groove

16th Dance

Dotted 8th Dance

Dotted 8th Jam

♩ = 72 - 96

What a Difference a Dot Makes

♩ = 88 - 112

3/4 Hymn

♩ = 100 - 124

3/4 With a Twist

♩ = 144 - 180

6/8 March

6/8 Dance

6/8 Frolic

Three in a Beat

What a Triplet

♩ = 88 - 112

1 vs 2 vs 3 vs 4

♩ = 92 - 116

A Somewhat Tricky Scale

♩ = 92 - 116

Syncopation Basics

♩ = 88 - 112

Syncopate This

♩ = 88 - 112

Syncopation Song

♩ = 88 - 112

Syncopation Nation

♩ = 108 - 132

Well-Known Melodies

"Sakura"

♩ = 84 - 108

Japanese Traditional

"American Patrol"

♩ = 84 - 108

Frank White Meacham

"Simple Gifts"

♩ = 100 - 124

Shaker Song

"We Three Kings"

♩. = 52 - 76

John Henry Hopkins, Jr.

"Happy Birthday"

♩ = 96 - 120

American Traditional

"Amazing Grace"

American Gospel

"Toreador March" from *Carmen*

Georges Bizet

"Over the River and Through the Woods"

American Folk Song

Well-Known Melodies

"When the Saints Go Marching In"

American Gospel

"Kum Ba Ya"

American Folk

"Yankee Doodle"

American Traditional

"America"

American Traditional
lyrics by Samuel Francis Smith

Theme from *Symphony No. 9 in E minor: IV. Allegro con fuoco*

Antonín Dvořák

Minuet in G Major

Johann Sebastian Bach

Well-Known Melodies

Theme from *Symphony No. 9 in E minor: II. Largo*

Antonín Dvořák

Bransle Quatre Bransles

Tielman Susato

"Auld Lang Syne"

♩ = 96 - 108

Scottish Traditional

"America the Beautiful"

♩ = 84 - 100

Samuel A. Ward
lyrics by Katharine Lee Bates

"Fum Fum Fum"

♩ = 108 - 124

Traditional Spanish Carol

Well-Known Melodies

"Home Sweet Home"

♩ = 108 - 124

Henry R. Bishop

"When Johnny Comes Marching Home"

♩. = 120 - 132

Patrick Gilmore
(a.k.a. Louis Lambert)

"La donna è mobile" from *Rigoletto*

Giuseppe Verdi

"Scarborough Fair"

English Traditional

Well-Known Melodies

"The Entertainer"

Scott Joplin

"Marche au Supplice" from *Symphonie Fantastique*

Hector Berlioz

Legato Studies

Fingering Sequence: 0 - 2 - 1 - 1,2 - 2,3 - 1,3 - 1,2,3 (and reverse)

16

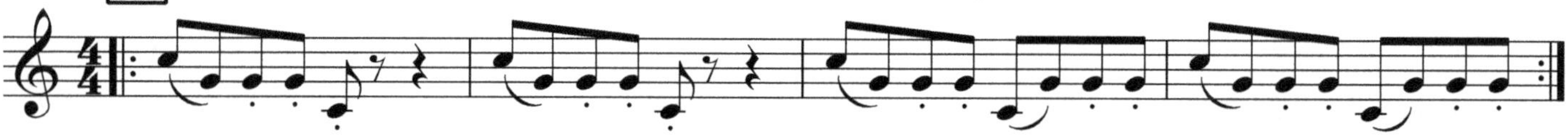

17

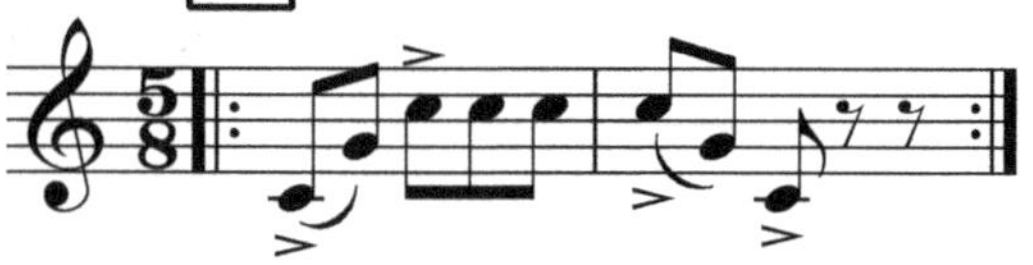

18

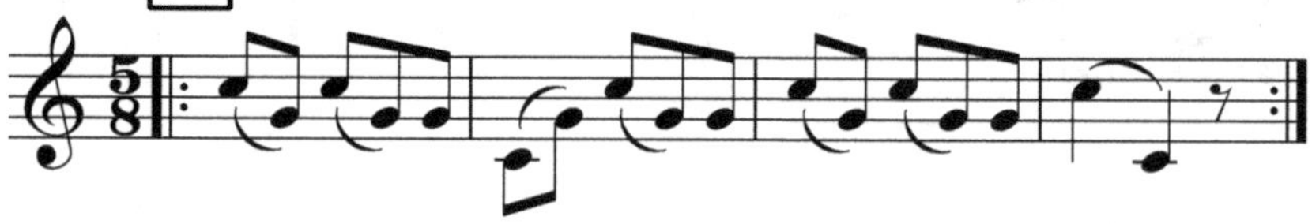

19

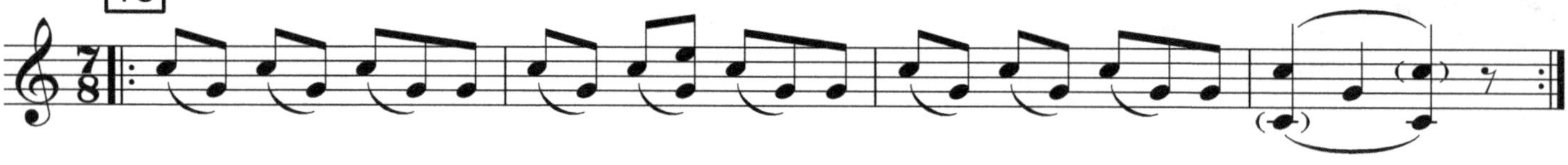

20

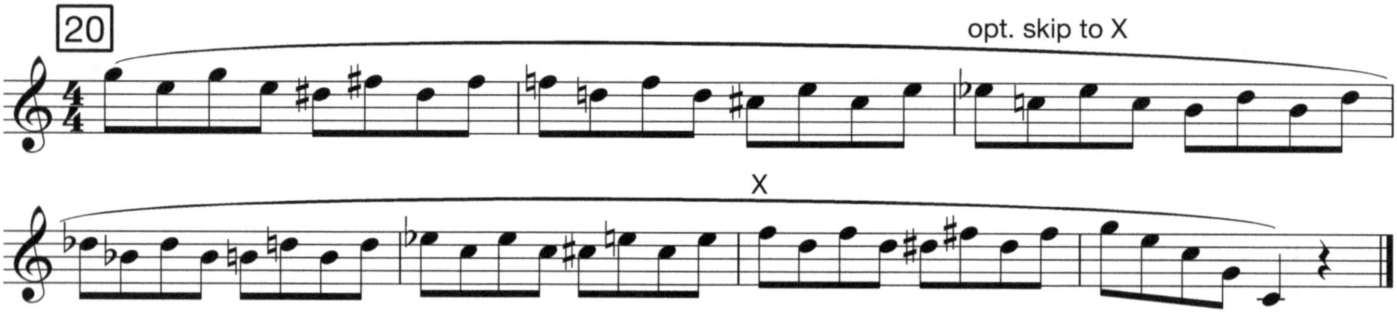

21

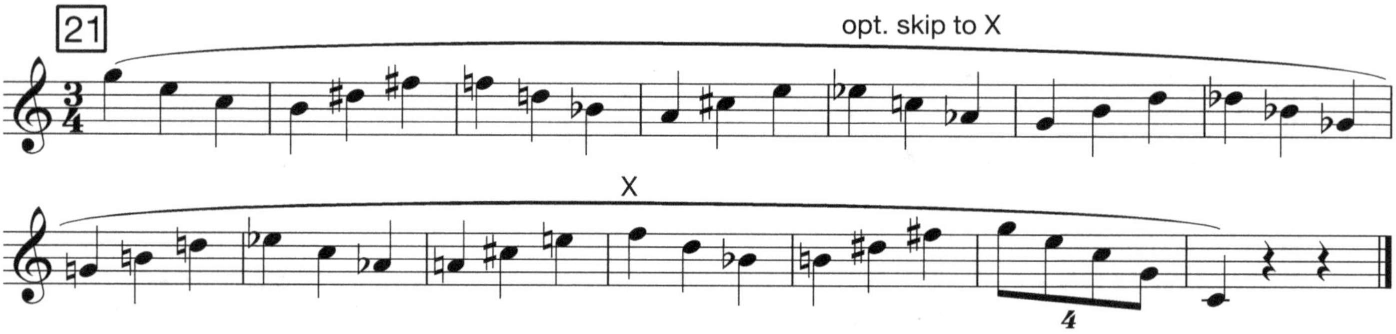

Appendix
Scale Degrees and Intervals

Scale Degrees

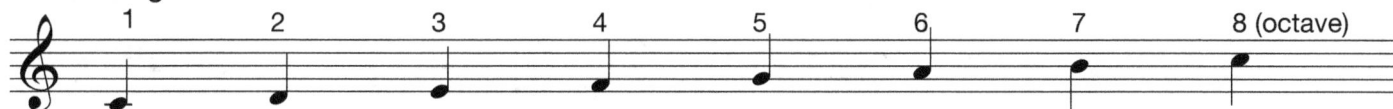

Numbering Intervals

An *interval* is numbered by how many scale degress it spans. For example, the *interval* spanned by three scale degrees is called a *third*.

If we go from C to E, we say we have gone "up a *third*."

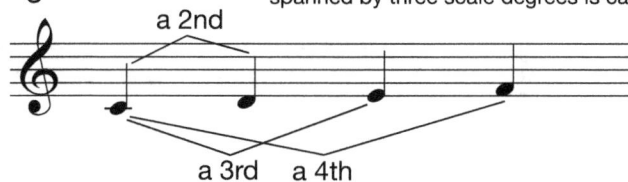

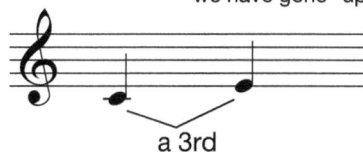

An *interval* is also the number of lines and spaces spanned by the two notes. For example, going from C to the G♭ encompasses 2 spaces and 3 lines, so we know that the interval is some kind of 5th (2+3=5).

some kind of 5th
(specific kind of 5th shown below)

General Intervals

prime   2nd   3rd   4th   5th   6th   7th   octave

Specific Intervals

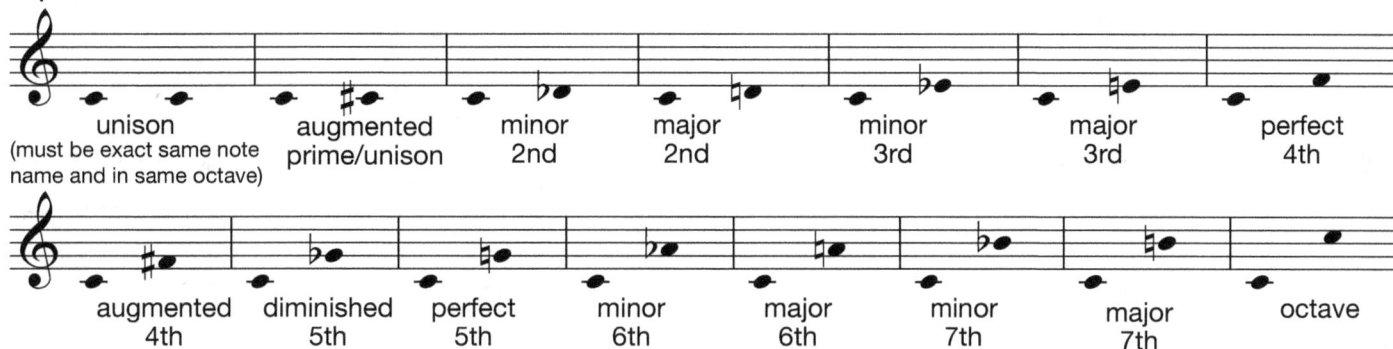

unison
(must be exact same note name and in same octave)   augmented prime/unison   minor 2nd   major 2nd   minor 3rd   major 3rd   perfect 4th

augmented 4th   diminished 5th   perfect 5th   minor 6th   major 6th   minor 7th   major 7th   octave

Half-steps and Whole-Steps

The interval between one tone and the next nearest tone can also be called a *half-step* or a *semitone*.

The interval between one tone and the tone that is two *half-steps* away can also be called a *whole-step*.

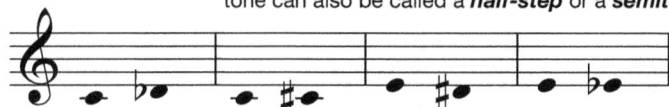

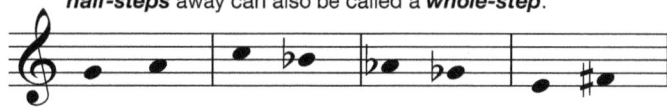

49

Relatives

Each **key signature** is shared by one major and one minor key, and the two are said to be **relative**.
For example, C major is the **relative major** of A minor, and A minor is the **relative minor** of C major.

C Major

A Minor

G Major

E Minor

D Major

B Minor

A Major

F# Minor

E Major

C# Minor

B Major

G# Minor

F# Major

D# Minor

C# Major
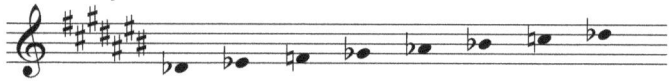

A# Minor

A♭ Major

F Minor

E♭ Major

C Minor

B♭ Major

G Minor

F Major

Notice how each minor key starts a 6th above (or a 3rd below) its relative major key.

D Minor
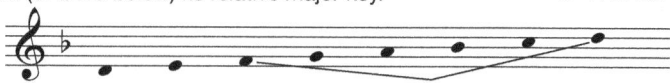

part of D minor

part of F major

50

Parallels

Keys with the same letter name are said to be *parallel*. For example, C major
is the *parallel major* of C minor, and C minor is the *parallel minor* of C major.

C Major    C Minor

The differences between the major and minor scales are the 3rd, 6th, and 7th scale degrees.

G Major    G Minor

D Major    D Minor

A Major    A Minor

E Major    E Minor

B Major    B Minor

F# Major    F# Minor

C# Major    C# Minor

Ab Major    Ab Minor

Eb Major    Eb Minor

Bb Major    Bb Minor

F Major    F Minor

Appendix

Other Scales

Chromatic Scale

A *chromatic scale* is a scale that moves by *half-steps*, sort of like pressing every key in order on a piano.

Whole-Tone Scale

A *whole-tone scale* is a scale that moves by *whole-steps.* The terms *whole-tone* and *whole-step* are used interchangeably.

Scale Ideas for Practicing Chromatic and Whole-Tone Scales

Glossary

accidental	a note that is not part of the scale or key indicated by the key signature; a symbol marking such a note - ♮, ♯, ♭, 𝄪, or 𝄫
chromatic	changing notes by half-steps or semitones; including notes that are not in the key signature
diatonic	only having notes that are in the key signature
enharmonic	a note that has the same pitch as another note, but that is spelled differently (e.g. A♯ and B♭)
embouchure	the shape and position of the lips while playing a wind instrument such as the trumpet
half-step	the interval between a pitch and the nearest possible pitch, above or below (e.g. C to the nearest C#, or D to the nearest Db); also known as a semitone
interval	the pitch distance between two notes; the number of letter names the distance spans (e.g. A to the E above is a fifth, spanning the five notes A, B, C, D, and E)
key signature	the part of the music staff that tells you which notes have sharps or flats
key	a phrase (e.g. "G major") naming the tonic and scale that has the notes the music will mostly use; (e.g. A simple piece in G major might use G, A, B, C, D, E, and F♯, and end on a G.)
measure	a unit of music between two vertical "bar lines"; also called a bar
note	a symbol indicating a tone to be played, how long you hold it, and a name for the tone made up of a letter, A through G, either by itself or with an accidental - ♮, ♯, ♭, 𝄪, or 𝄫
octave	the interval that spans a note and the next nearest note with the *exact* same name
parallel	having the same tonic note but in a different mode (e.g. C major and C minor are parallels)
pitch	the actual sound of a note (B and C♭ are the same pitch, but not the same note.)
relative	having the same key signature but a different tonic (e.g. C major and A minor are relatives)
scale degree	a note's position in a scale, starting with the tonic as scale degree 1
tempo	the pace of the music, described by a word or phrase or by a number showing how many beats there are per minute
time signature	a symbol telling you how many beats are in each measure and what note value is counted as a beat (e.g. "3/4" means three beats per measure and the quarter-note gets one beat)
tonic	the focus or main note of a key or scale; also called the key-note; the music will seem to "pull toward" this note and sound complete when ending on it (e.g. The tonic of C major is C.)
whole-step	an interval made up of two half-steps or semitones (e.g. from C up to the nearest D, or from F down to the nearest E♭); also called a whole-tone

Appendix

Suggestions

- You might try playing a major scale and then immediately playing its relative minor scale. For example, play C major on page 4 followed by A minor on page 16. Then G major followed by E minor, and so on. This could help reinforce your understanding of how major and minor keys share key signatures and relate to each other.

- Once you're comfortable with each scale in a study, play the entire study as one exercise. For example, on Study 2.3, start with the C Major scale and play through each double-bar line, keeping steady tempo, until you reach the final bar line on the next page.

- After learning a scale in a comfortable octave, play the same scale in a different octave. Playing scales can be useful for extending your comfortable range, both high and low.

- If you're a beginner, use the simpler scales and arpeggios, especially those in Part 1, to develop a solid sound and embouchure. Sound and embouchure issues are difficult things to fix later on.

- Always change notes with as little change in your lips as possible. Notes may *look* far apart on printed music, but this does not mean that they are far apart on your embouchure or that an interval requires a large shift in lip tension.

- For each scale, pick a tempo that allows you to play every note and rhythm accurately while keeping the tempo steady. Then, gradually increase the tempo from there.

- Use a metronome when you practice. Even though a lot of the music you play will not have strict tempo, you want to be able to have as much control of your rhythm and timing as possible. You want any tempo fluctuations to be *your* tempo fluctuations, and not just random results of poor technique. Metronome work can give you that control.

- Record yourself. This will let you hear some aspects of your playing you might not notice while you are playing, such as unwanted tempo fluctuations or a note that doesn't sound quite as nice the others you played.

- Use a mirror. While it might not be worthwhile to obsess over having a perfect embouchure, periodically watching yourself play in a mirror can help you catch some bad habits, such as unnecessarily tilting the instrument or playing with it pointing off at a significant angle.

- Use a tuner and a pitch source. A tuner is good for pointing out which tones you tend to play sharp or flat, and can also show you any tones that you may have "gotten used to" playing out of tune and which now sound in tune to you. A pitch source, such as any device playing a sustained drone, can be useful for you to hear how your trumpet playing mixes with other musical sounds around you.

- Rest whenever you need to. It's important to "push it" sometimes and build endurance, but if you find yourself forcing something or muscling something because you are tired, then it's time to rest. Forceful playing will not be how you ultimately want to play, so there's no reason to risk that becoming a habit.

- Don't force anything. Brass playing is much more about accuracy, finesse, and finding the "sweet spot" of every note than it is about strength and power. Even though some strengthening is required to play the trumpet, sheer muscle power rarely works.

Additional Information:

Please visit ***www.takecenterstage.today*** for more information on supplemental materials and upcoming books. If you have any questions or comments about this book, feel free to e-mail info@takecenterstage.today.

www.ingramcontent.com/pod-product-compliance
Lightning Source LLC
Chambersburg PA
CBHW081524040426

42447CB00013B/3337